good deeds

MB Macaw BOOKS

© Macaw Books

All rights reserved. No part of this publication may be reproduced or utilized in any form or by any means, electronic or mechanical including photocopying, recording or by any information storage and retrieval system without prior permission in writing from the publisher.

www.macawbooks.com

Printed in India

One morning,

Gilly woke up and looked

out of the window. The sun was shining brightly.

She smiled said aloud, 'It is such a beautiful day.

I will make it more beautiful with my good deeds.'

And so, Gilly set about doing her first good deed.

Gilly made some orange juice, eggs and bread.

Then she served Mummy breakfast in bed.

Then she filled a plate with nuts for her squirrel named Chucky. He chattered happily as he the nuts.

'Gilly went for a walk. There she helped a blind man cross the street. He thanked her and Gilly felt very glad.

Gilly decided to take a ride on the bus. There she offered a tired lady her seat on the bus. The lady smiled warmly at Gilly.

When Gilly got off the bus, she saw a girl who looked very sad. She gave the girl a hug and cheered her up.

Then Gilly met a boy who was very hungry. He did not have the money to buy food. Gilly shared her lunch with him.

Gilly was about to reach her home when she saw a cat caught in a tree. She climbed up the tree and rescued the cat.

Then Gilly saw a parrot. It looked very sad inside its cage.

Gilly quickly opened the cage and let it fly away.

Soon Gilly was home. She wrote a loving letter to her aunt who lived far away. 'I am sure aunt will love it,' Gilly thought.

Then Gilly went to visit old Mrs Davis who lived next door. She talked with the old lady and fed her some soup. 'Oh what a kind child you are,' said old Mrs Davis.

When Gilly went home that day, she was very tired. But she did not mind at all.

She decided to rest for a while before going back to her books. She now had a lot of stories to share with her friends.

And then, Gilly heard the sound of dogs barking. It was her brother, Jimmy with two pups. He told her that they were lost and hungry. Gilly smiled and said, 'Well what a good deed! Let's try to find who owns them.'And so Gilly set out on another adventure to do good deeds.

One morning Sally looked around her room and thought, 'Oh, my room is a mess.'

'I wonder when
I put everything
out of place.'

Sally's clothes were scattered on the bed.

Her shoes and toys were lying on the floor.

And her study table. Oh dear! What a sight it was.

The shelves were covered with dust, she had not cleaned them for so long.

And there were toffee wrappers lying all around. Sally loved to eat toffees but she forgot that there was a dustbin.

And then! TRIIIIIIING.....TRIIIIING!

'Oh no! Looks like we have a visitor. I have to clean my room before anyone enters it,' thought Sally.

Sally ran back to her room. She began with her clothes. She folded them neatly and kept them in the wardrobe.

She looked through her books and kept away the ones that she did not want any more.

Sally picked her toys and kept them away.

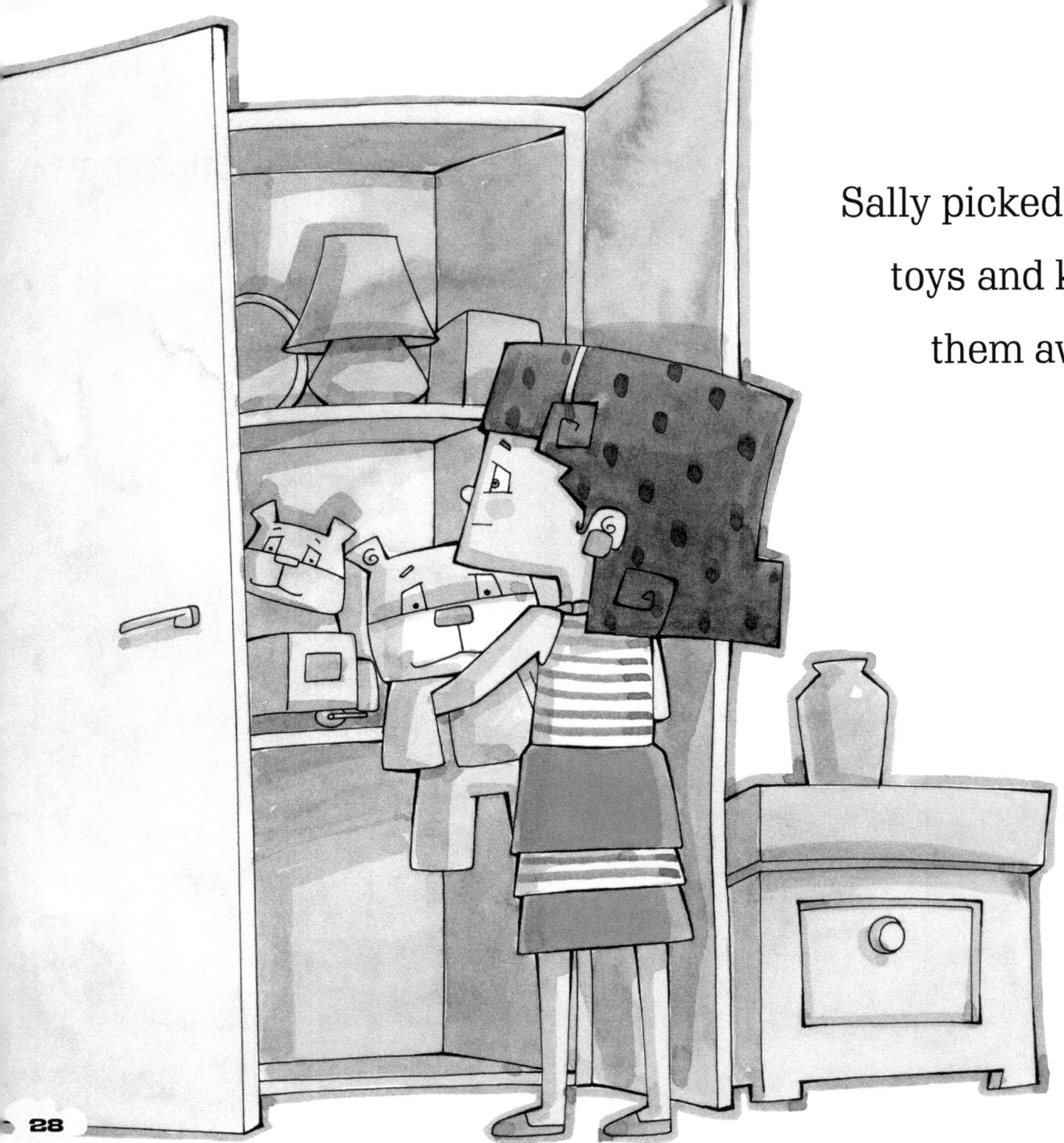

She opened her shoe rack and
stacked her shoes in a neat row.

Sally looked around and was very happy. 'Now all I need is a broom and a mop,' she said aloud.

And so she brought the broom and swept away the dust on the floor. Then she used the mop to wipe the floor clean.

Sally's room shone. It had never looked so clean. She was very happy. 'It feels so good. I will always keep my room clean,' Sally promised herself.

www.ingramcontent.com/pod-product-compliance
Lightning Source LLC
LaVergne TN
LVHW082324080426
835508LV00042B/1529